Times Table Mini-Books & Lift-n-Look Flash Cards

Reproducible Learning Tools That Make Mastering the Multiplication Facts Fun, Fun, Fun!

by Mary Beth Spann

SCHOLASTIC
PROFESSIONAL BOOKS

NEW YORK • TORONTO • LONDON • AUCKLAND • SYDNEY
MEXICO CITY • NEW DELHI • HONG KONG

Cover and Interior design by Jaime Lucero
Illustrations by Dave Clegg and Kate Flanagan
Characters and rhymes by Joseph D'Agnese and Jack Silbert

ISBN # 0-439-10438-6

Table of Contents

Times Table Mini-Books

Lift-n-Look Flash Cards

Introduction

 earning to recite multiplication tables is a near-legendary rite of passage in elementary school. I remember sitting beside my dad at our kitchen table when I was 8 years old, trying to recall and recite those mandatory "times tables." I'm not sure I even understood the concept behind multiplication. I only remember wishing the endless exercises would end.

Happily, we can help today's students approach the task of learning multiplication tables with confidence. As educators, we know that multiplication is closely related to addition. In fact, multiplication is easier to visualize and compute than simple subtraction, which has always been taught before multiplication. We now also realize the importance of providing children with concrete exercises in which they add same-size addends to introduce the concept of multiplication.

When the time does come for students to memorize multiplication tables, there are many ways to make that process easy and enjoyable, such as this collection of reproducible Times Table Mini-Books and Lift-n-Look Flash Cards. In this book, you'll find one mini-book and one flash card for each "times table," from 1 to 12. The mini-books introduce charming characters that will help students visualize the numbers they're multiplying. The Lift-n-Look Flash Cards provide kids with easy and portable self-testers they can use for a quick review. Plus, children will love the quirky cartoon that unfolds as they open the flaps that reveal the answers on each flash card.

Typically, the teacher-resource books I write are inspired by my own teaching needs or by those of my colleagues. But this book was inspired by my needs as a mom! To help my third-grade daughter, Francesca, learn her multiplication tables, I recorded the tables on mini-charts that she could use to drill herself. Through experimenting, I discovered that each multiplication table fits into an 8-page mini-book as well as a single-page lift-and-look device. We've found that the mini-books and flash cards are perfect for last-minute self-drill at the breakfast table or on the bus. Francesca loves their portability—they are small enough to tuck into her pocket or backpack.

I hope you and your students will appreciate adding these enjoyable multiplication devices to your math program. I wish I had these when I was 8 years old, faced with the daunting task of memorizing my multiplication tables!

Mary Beth Spann

About the Times Table Mini-Books

xxxxxxxxxxxxxxxxxxxxxxxxxxxxxxxxxxxxxxxxxxxxxxxxxxxxxxxxxxxxxxxxxxxxxxxxxxxxxxxxxxxxxxxxxxxx

The cover of each multiplication mini-book stars a delightful character who displays a number of items. Using rhyme and humor, the character makes learning the times table fun and easy. The character also appears inside the mini-book to illustrate each multiplication sentence. For example, a turtle balancing three teacups introduces "The 3 Times Table." One turtle represents 1 set of 3 teacups, or 1 x 3 = 3. Two turtles depict 2 sets of 3 teacups: 2 x 3 = 6, and so on.

Below is a complete list of the characters and their "belongings" as represented in the Times Table Mini-Books:

1	Times Table:	Willy Worm with 1 hat
2	Times Table:	Tina Tuna with 2 boats
3	Times Table:	Teddy Turtle with 3 teacups
4	Times Table:	Flo Flamingo with 4 pizza pies
5	Times Table:	Fernando Frog with 5 trampolines
6	Times Table:	Sally Seahorse with 6 sunflowers
7	Times Table:	Skippy Skunk with 7 perfume bottles
8	Times Table:	Amy Ape with 8 footballs
9	Times Table:	Norman Newt with 9 ties
10	Times Table:	Tonya Turkey with 10 bowling pins
11	Times Table:	Elvis Elk with 11 spoons
12	Times Table:	Tillie Tiger with 12 eggs

Making the Times Table Mini-Books

1. Carefully remove the mini-book to be copied, tearing along the perforation.

2. Make a double-sided copy of the mini-book for each student. If your machine doesn't have a double-sided function, photocopy the first page of the mini-book. (Make extra copies in case of mistakes.) Then place the copies blank side up into the machine's paper tray. Next, make a test copy of the second page to make sure that the pages on both sides are aligned correctly. Check your double-sided copy against the original page.

3. Have students cut their mini-book along the dotted line. Then have them fold the top half so that the title page faces out, and the bottom half so that page 3 faces out. Nestle page 3 inside the title page and staple the mini-book together.

4. Encourage children to color the characters in the mini-book.

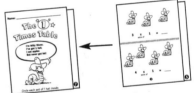

Using the Times Table Mini-Books

1. Begin by distributing copies of The 1 Times Table. Help students cut, fold, and assemble their mini-book (see directions above). Then have each child add his or her name on the line provided.

2. Look at the mini-book cover together. Help children focus on the character on the cover (Willy Worm) and his item (hat). Ask students: How many hats does Willy Worm have? (*One*) Inform students that each worm they'll see wears 1 set of 1 hat.

3. Open the book to the second page and invite kids to read aloud the first math sentence: 0 x 1 = 0. Ask: How many worms do you see above this sentence? (*Zero*) How many hats are there? (*Zero*) So the product equals zero.

4. Ask students: How many sets of hats would there be if there's only one Willy Worm? (*One*) How many hats are there in each set? (*One*) So, 1 set of 1 equals 1. Draw one worm with a hat on the board. Under it write:

$$1 \underset{\text{set of}}{\text{ x }} 1 = 1$$

5. Now draw a second Willy Worm on the board. Ask students: How many worms do you see? (*Two*) How many hats does each worm have? (*One*) How many hats are there in all? (*Two*) Under the worms write: $2 \underset{\text{sets of}}{\text{ x }} 1 = 2.$

6 Have students look inside their mini-book. Invite them to count the sets of 1 hat by drawing a circle around each worm. Then have them fill in the blank below each picture with the appropriate product. (You can either continue doing this as a whole-class activity, or encourage students to work together in small groups.)

7 When children have completed filling in their mini-books, challenge them to work individually to answer the review activity on the back page. Students can check their answers against the multiplication facts inside the mini-book.

8 Repeat Steps 1 to 7 as you introduce children to the other multiplication mini-books. Continue to stress the notion that each character represents one set of the number of objects he or she holds. For example, in The 2 Times Table mini-book, ask students: How many boats does Tina Tuna have? *(Two)* Remind students that this means Tina Tuna owns 1 set of 2 boats. If there were two tunas, how many sets of boats would there be? *(Two)* If there were 2 sets of 2 boats, how many boats would there be in all? *(Four)*

9 Encourage students to keep the mini-book they are working on for as long as they need. As students complete each mini-book and memorize its contents, have them tell you when they're ready to be "tested." You can then meet with each student one at a time and listen to him or her recite the target table without referring to the mini-book. You may also want to pose problems to the student in random order and with factors inverted. Make yourself available for a few moments of class time each day for this purpose.

10 When a student can correctly recite a particular times table, reward his or her efforts by affixing a sticker to the mini-book's cover. Then help the student punch a hole in the mini-book and slip it onto a metal loose-leaf ring. Students can gauge their own progress as they add other completed mini-books to their ring.

Management and Storage Tips

○ Get 12 file folders and label the folder tabs "1 Times Table Mini-Book," "2 Times Table Mini-Book," etc. Store a class set of each multiplication mini-book in its corresponding folder until students are ready to use them.

○ Place the folders in a plastic bin or box. (TIP: You may want to offer children the easiest-to-learn tables first [i.e., the 1's, 2's, 5's, and 10's tables] before letting them tackle the more difficult ones. Place the folders in the order you want students to master the tables.)

○ Attach a class list inside the front cover of each folder so that you can check off the names of students who have completed the corresponding mini-book. Or keep a master list of student names and mini-books in a separate folder on your desk.

Student	1x Table	2x Table	3x Table	4x Table	5x Table
Rosa	✓	✓			✓
Thanh	✓	✓	✓		
Jerrod	✓	✓	✓	✓	
Anna	✓	✓	✓		✓
Ben	✓	✓			

○ Set up an accessible storage system for the completed mini-books. Use a shoebox, the pockets of a plastic shoe bag, or a multi-hook hanger (for belts or scarves) to store or hang students' collections. Place this storage system near the unused mini-book folder bin.

About the Lift-n-Look Flash Cards

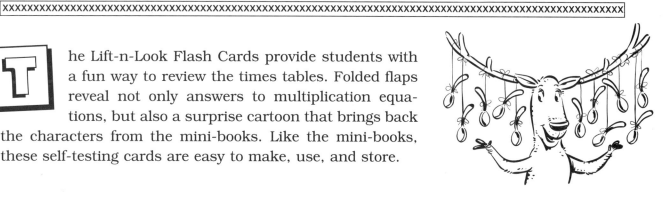

he Lift-n-Look Flash Cards provide students with a fun way to review the times tables. Folded flaps reveal not only answers to multiplication equations, but also a surprise cartoon that brings back the characters from the mini-books. Like the mini-books, these self-testing cards are easy to make, use, and store.

Making the Lift-n-Look Flash Cards

1 Carefully remove the Lift-n-Look card to be copied, tearing along the perforation.

2 Make a copy of the card for each student.

3 Have students glue the page to construction paper and let it dry. Then have them cut along the solid lines. Fold over the dotted lines to create flaps that open and close. Kids can use small paper clips to hold the flaps down.

4 Encourage children to color or decorate their cards.

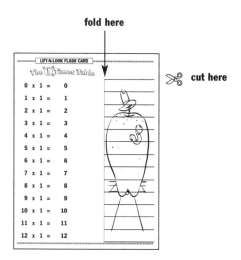

Using the Lift-n-Look Flash Cards

1 Distribute the Lift-n-Look cards to students. Help them make the cards (see directions above).

2 Have students leave the flaps open and invite them to read aloud the equations on the card. This is one way kids can memorize the multiplication table.

3 Guide students to discover multiplication's *commutative property*—they can reverse the factors but the product remains the same. Compare the number sentence "2 x 1 = 2" in the 1's table with the number sentence "1 x 2 = 2" in the 2's table.

4 Demonstrate to students how they can also use the cards to quiz themselves: Keeping the flaps closed, kids can guess the answer to an equation. Then they can open the

flap to check their answer. Encourage students to drill themselves in different ways: lifting the flaps from top to bottom, from bottom to top, or in random order. Students can also use the flash cards to review the tables with a partner.

Management and Storage Tips

O Get 12 file folders and label the folder tabs "1 Times Table Lift-n-Look," "2 Times Table Lift-n-Look," etc. Store a class set of each multiplication flash card in its corresponding folder until students are ready to use them.

O Place the folders in a plastic bin or box. As with the mini-book folders, you may want to store each flash-card folder in the order in which you wish students to master them.

O Create a multiplication learning center in your classroom. Store the flash-card folders, mini-book folders, mini-book ring collections, multiplication manipulatives, teacher resource books, and art supplies here.

1 TIMES TABLE MINI-REVIEW

2 x 1 = _____
11 x 1 = _____
7 x 1 = _____
5 x 1 = _____
8 x 1 = _____
10 x 1 = _____
9 x 1 = _____
4 x 1 = _____
1 x 1 = _____
6 x 1 = _____
3 x 1 = _____
12 x 1 = _____

❽

The ① Times Table

> I'm Willy Worm.
> I've got 1 hat;
> I eat apples
> But never get fat!

Circle each set of 1 hat inside.

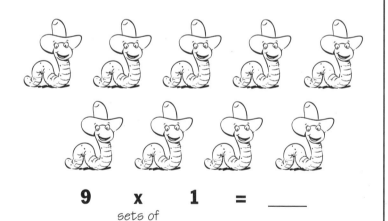

9 x 1 = _____
sets of

3 x 1 = _____
sets of

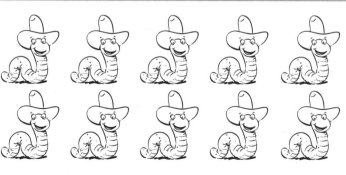

10 x 1 = _____
sets of

❻

4 x 1 = _____
sets of

❸

0   x   **1**   =   **0**
set of

11   x   **1**   =   ___
sets of

1   x   **1**   =   ___
set of

12   x   **1**   =   ___
sets of

❼

2   x   **1**   =   ___
sets of

❷

5   x   **1**   =   ___
sets of

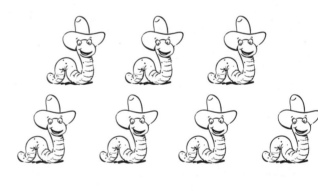

7   x   **1**   =   ___
sets of

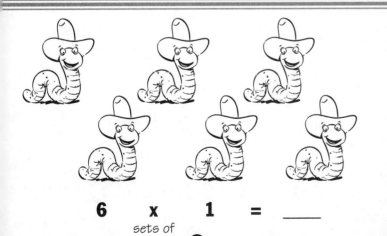

6   x   **1**   =   ___
sets of

❹

8   x   **1**   =   ___
sets of

❺

2 TIMES TABLE MINI-REVIEW

1   x   2   =   ____
10   x   2   =   ____
3   x   2   =   ____
12   x   2   =   ____
6   x   2   =   ____
11   x   2   =   ____
7   x   2   =   ____
5   x   2   =   ____
9   x   2   =   ____
8   x   2   =   ____
2   x   2   =   ____
4   x   2   =   ____

The ② Times Table

I'm Tina Tuna.
I've got 2 boats;
When I'm not swimming
I like to float.

Circle each set of 2 boats inside.

9   x   2   =   ____
sets of

10   x   2   =   ____
sets of

3   x   2   =   ____
sets of

4   x   2   =   ____
sets of

0   x   **2**   =   **0**
set of

1   x   **2**   =   ___
set of

2   x   **2**   =   ___
sets of

❷

5   x   **2**   =   ___
sets of

6   x   **2**   =   ___
sets of

❹

11   x   **2**   =   ___
sets of

12   x   **2**   =   ___
sets of

❼

7   x   **2**   =   ___
sets of

8   x   **2**   =   ___
sets of

❺

3 TIMES TABLE MINI-REVIEW

8 x 3 = ____
2 x 3 = ____
4 x 3 = ____
3 x 3 = ____
11 x 3 = ____
7 x 3 = ____
5 x 3 = ____
9 x 3 = ____
10 x 3 = ____
1 x 3 = ____
12 x 3 = ____
6 x 3 = ____

8

Name: _____

The ③ Times Table

I'm Teddy Turtle.
I've got 3 teacups.
I like tea
But it gives me hiccups!

Circle each set of 3 teacups inside.

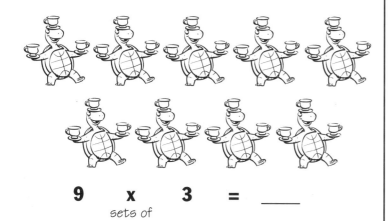

9 x 3 = ____
sets of

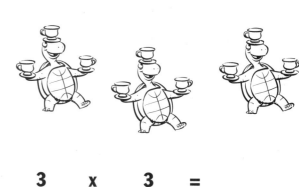

3 x 3 = ____
sets of

10 x 3 = ____
sets of

6

4 x 3 = ____
sets of

3

0   x   **3**   =   **0**
set of

1   x   **3**   =   ___
set of

2   x   **3**   =   ___
sets of

❷

5   x   **3**   =   ___
sets of

6   x   **3**   =   ___
sets of

❹

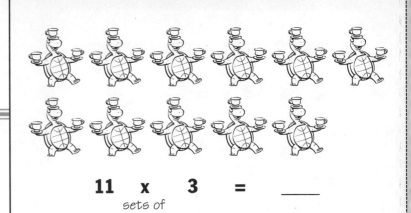

11   x   **3**   =   ___
sets of

12 x   **3**   =   ___
sets of

❼

7   x   **3**   =   ___
sets of

8   x   **3**   =   ___
sets of

❺

4 TIMES TABLE MINI-REVIEW

1 x 4 = _____

11 x 4 = _____

9 x 4 = _____

5 x 4 = _____

10 x 4 = _____

7 x 4 = _____

8 x 4 = _____

12 x 4 = _____

6 x 4 = _____

2 x 4 = _____

4 x 4 = _____

3 x 4 = _____

8

Name: _____

The ④ Times Table

I'm Flo Flamingo.
I've got 4 pizza pies;
I like them better
Than burgers and fries.

Circle each set of 4 pizzas inside.

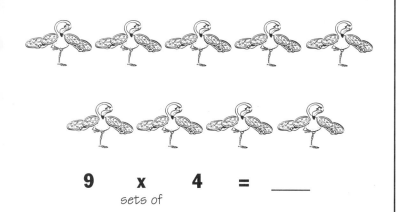

9 x 4 = _____
sets of

3 x 4 = _____
sets of

10 x 4 = _____
sets of

6

4 x 4 = _____
sets of

3

0   **x**   **4**   **=**   **0**
set of

1   **x**   **4**   **=**   ____
set of

2   **x**   **4**   **=**   ____
sets of

❷

5   **x**   **4**   **=**   ____
sets of

6   **x**   **4**   **=**   ____
sets of

❹

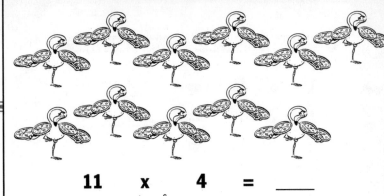

11   **x**   **4**   **=**   ____
sets of

12   **x**   **4**   **=**   ____
sets of

❼

7   **x**   **4**   **=**   ____
sets of

8   **x**   **4**   **=**   ____
sets of

❺

5 TIMES TABLE MINI-REVIEW

6 x 5 = ____
8 x 5 = ____
7 x 5 = ____
9 x 5 = ____
10 x 5 = ____
5 x 5 = ____
12 x 5 = ____
4 x 5 = ____
2 x 5 = ____
1 x 5 = ____
3 x 5 = ____
11 x 5 = ____

Name: _____

The (5) Times Table

I'm Fernando Frog.
I've got 5 trampolines;
They help me hop
Just like jumping beans!

Circle each set of 5 trampolines inside.

9 x 5 = ____
sets of

3 x 5 = ____
sets of

10 x 5 = ____
sets of

4 x 5 = ____
sets of

0   **x**   **5**   **=**   **0**
set of

11   **x**   **5**   **=**   ___
sets of

1   **x**   **5**   **=**   ___
set of

12   **x**   **5**   **=**   ___
sets of

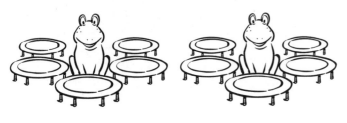

2   **x**   **5**   **=**   ___
sets of

❷

❼

5   **x**   **5**   **=**   ___
sets of

7   **x**   **5**   **=**   ___
sets of

6   **x**   **5**   **=**   ___
sets of

❹

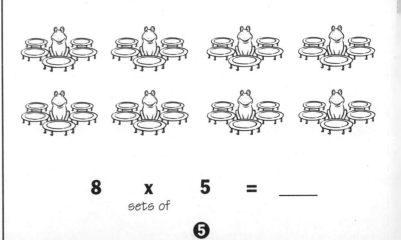

8   **x**   **5**   **=**   ___
sets of

❺

6 TIMES TABLE MINI-REVIEW

8	x	6	=	_____
5	x	6	=	_____
11	x	6	=	_____
7	x	6	=	_____
2	x	6	=	_____
9	x	6	=	_____
4	x	6	=	_____
6	x	6	=	_____
1	x	6	=	_____
3	x	6	=	_____
10	x	6	=	_____
12	x	6	=	_____

8

Name: _____

The ⑥ Times Table

I'm Sally Seahorse.
I've got 6 sunflowers;
I like to water them
For hours and hours.

Circle each set of 6 sunflowers inside.

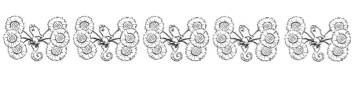

9   x   6   = ____
sets of

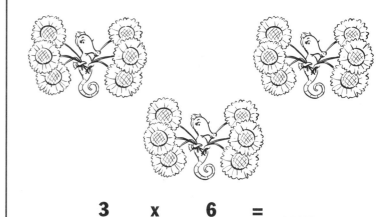

3   x   6   = ____
sets of

10   x   6   = ____
sets of

6

4   x   6   = ____
sets of

3

0   **x**   **6**   **=**   **0**
set of

11   **x**   **6**   **=**   ____
sets of

1   **x**   **6**   **=**   ____
set of

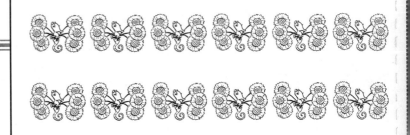

12   **x**   **6**   **=**   ____
sets of

❼

2   **x**   **6**   **=**   ____
sets of

❷

5   **x**   **6**   **=**   ____
sets of

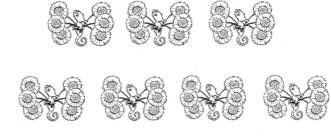

7   **x**   **6**   **=**   ____
sets of

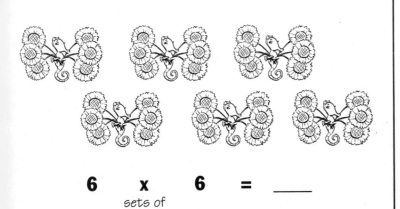

6   **x**   **6**   **=**   ____
sets of

❹

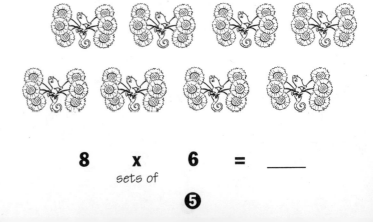

8   **x**   **6**   **=**   ____
sets of

❺

7 TIMES TABLE MINI-REVIEW

7 x 7 = ____
9 x 7 = ____
11 x 7 = ____
5 x 7 = ____
1 x 7 = ____
2 x 7 = ____
8 x 7 = ____
4 x 7 = ____
10 x 7 = ____
6 x 7 = ____
3 x 7 = ____
12 x 7 = ____

❽

The ⑦ Times Table

I'm Skippy Skunk.
I've got 7 bottles of perfume.
I use them so I don't
Stink up the room!

Circle each set of 7 perfume bottles inside.

3 x 7 = ____
sets of

❸

9 x 7 = ____
sets of

10 x 7 = ____
sets of

❻

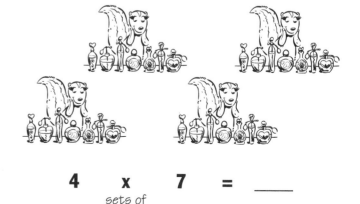

4 x 7 = ____
sets of

0   **x**   **7**   **=**   **0**
set of

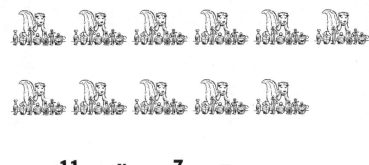

11   **x**   **7**   **=**   ____
sets of

1   **x**   **7**   **=**   ____
set of

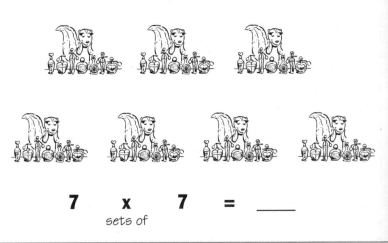

12   **x**   **7**   **=**   ____
sets of

2   **x**   **7**   **=**   ____
sets of

❷

❼

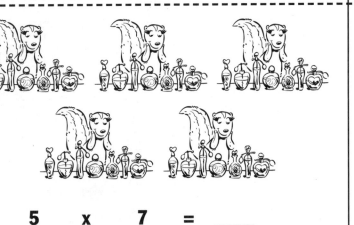

5   **x**   **7**   **=**   ____
sets of

7   **x**   **7**   **=**   ____
sets of

6   **x**   **7**   **=**   ____
sets of

❹

8   **x**   **7**   **=**   ____
sets of

❺

8 TIMES TABLE MINI-REVIEW

11 x 8 = ____
7 x 8 = ____
5 x 8 = ____
9 x 8 = ____
8 x 8 = ____
2 x 8 = ____
4 x 8 = ____
1 x 8 = ____
10 x 8 = ____
3 x 8 = ____
12 x 8 = ____
6 x 8 = ____

❽

The ⑧ Times Table

I'm Amy Ape.
I've got 8 footballs.
I like to bounce them
Off the walls.

Circle each set of 8 footballs inside.

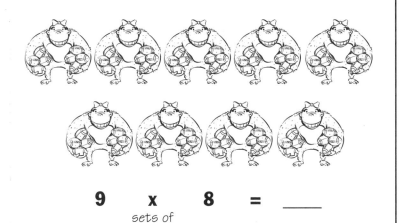

9 x 8 = ____
sets of

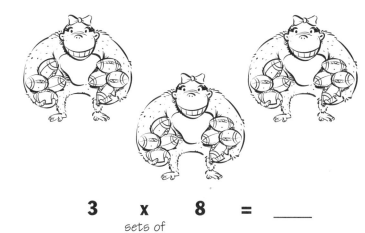

3 x 8 = ____
sets of

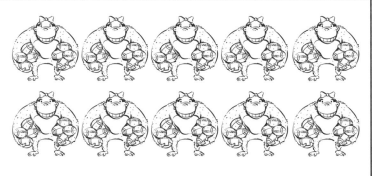

10 x 8 = ____
sets of

❻

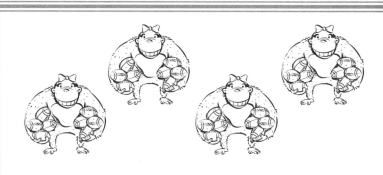

4 x 8 = ____
sets of

❸

0 x **8** = **0**
set of

1 x **8** = ___
set of

2 x **8** = ___
sets of

❷

11 x **8** = ___
sets of

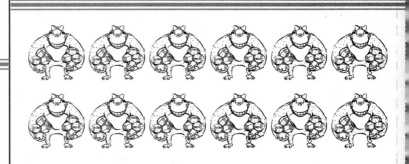

12 x **8** = ___
sets of

❼

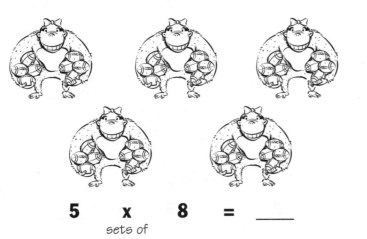

5 x **8** = ___
sets of

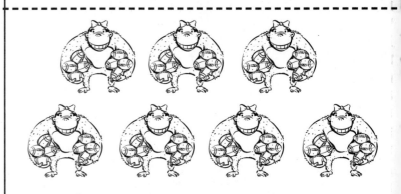

7 x **8** = ___
sets of

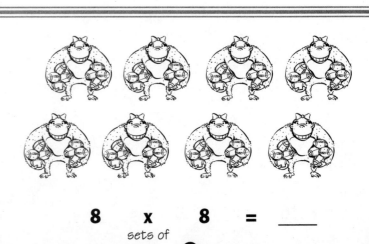

6 x **8** = ___
sets of

❹

8 x **8** = ___
sets of

❺

9 TIMES TABLE MINI-REVIEW

5 x 9 = _____
9 x 9 = _____
11 x 9 = _____
7 x 9 = _____
8 x 9 = _____
2 x 9 = _____
4 x 9 = _____
1 x 9 = _____
10 x 9 = _____
3 x 9 = _____
12 x 9 = _____
6 x 9 = _____

Name: _____

The 9 Times Table

I'm Norman Newt.
I've got 9 ties;
Each one a different
Color and size!

Circle each set of 9 ties inside.

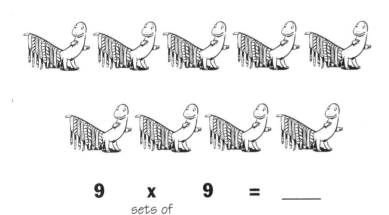

9   x   9   = _____
sets of

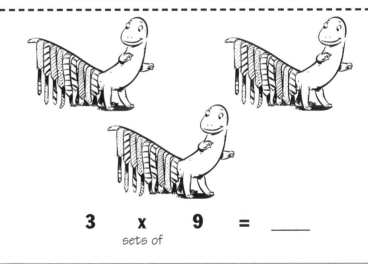

3   x   9   = _____
sets of

10   x   9   = _____
sets of

4   x   9   = _____
sets of

0 x **9** = **0**
set of

1 x **9** = ___
set of

2 x **9** = ___
sets of

❷

5 x **9** = ___
sets of

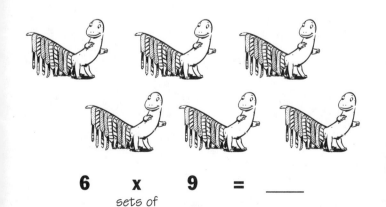

6 x **9** = ___
sets of

❹

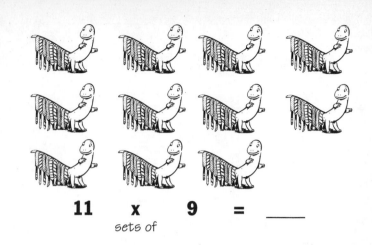

11 x **9** = ___
sets of

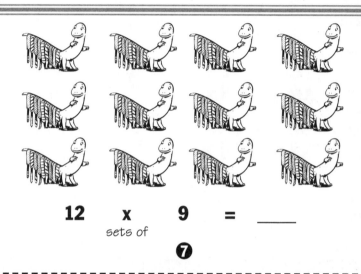

12 x **9** = ___
sets of

❼

7 x **9** = ___
sets of

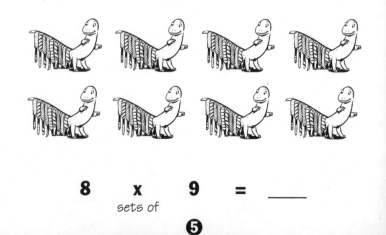

8 x **9** = ___
sets of

❺

10 TIMES TABLE MINI-REVIEW

10 x 10 = _____
7 x 10 = _____
5 x 10 = _____
9 x 10 = _____
8 x 10 = _____
2 x 10 = _____
4 x 10 = _____
1 x 10 = _____
12 x 10 = _____
3 x 10 = _____
11 x 10 = _____
6 x 10 = _____

8

The 10 Times Table

I'm Tonya Turkey.
I've got 10 bowling pins;
I knock them down
And my team wins!

Circle each set of 10 bowling pins inside.

9 x 10 = _____
sets of

3 x 10 = _____
sets of

10 x 10 = _____
sets of

6

4 x 10 = _____
sets of

3

0　　x　　**10**　　=　　**0**
set of

11　　x　　**10**　　=　　____
sets of

1　　x　　**10**　　=　　____
set of

12　　x　　**10**　　=　　____
sets of

❼

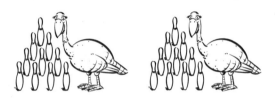

2　　x　　**10**　　=　　____
sets of

❷

5　　x　　**10**　　=　　____
sets of

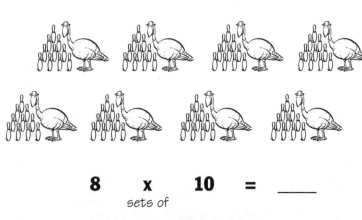

7　　x　　**10**　　=　　____
sets of

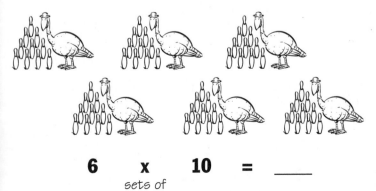

6　　x　　**10**　　=　　____
sets of

❹

8　　x　　**10**　　=　　____
sets of

❺

11 TIMES TABLE MINI-REVIEW

7 x 11 = ____
5 x 11 = ____
9 x 11 = ____
11 x 11 = ____
8 x 11 = ____
2 x 11 = ____
12 x 11 = ____
3 x 11 = ____
10 x 11 = ____
4 x 11 = ____
1 x 11 = ____
6 x 11 = ____

❽

Name: _____

The ⑪ Times Table

I'm Elvis Elk.
I've got 11 spoons;
I wear them on my head
To scare away raccoons!

Circle each set of 11 spoons inside.

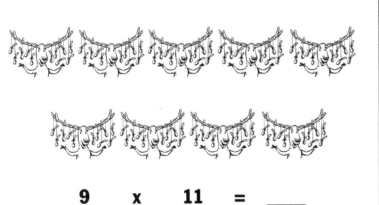

9 x 11 = ____
sets of

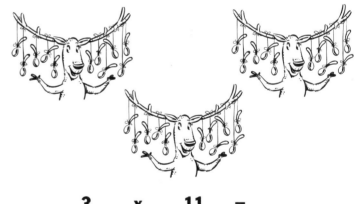

3 x 11 = ____
sets of

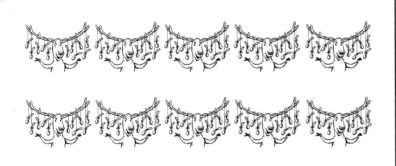

10 x 11 = ____
sets of

❻

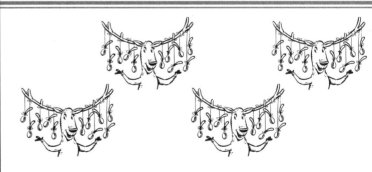

4 x 11 = ____
sets of

❸

0 x **11** = **0**
set of

1 x **11** = ___
set of

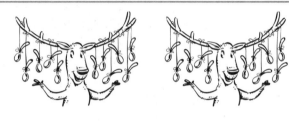

2 x **11** = ___
sets of

❷

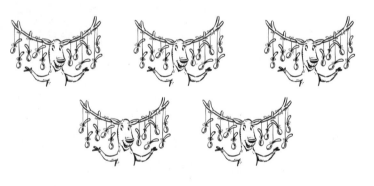

5 x **11** = ___
sets of

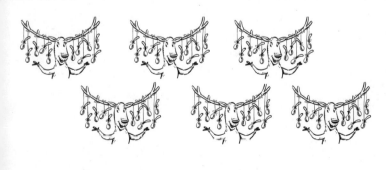

6 x **11** = ___
sets of

❹

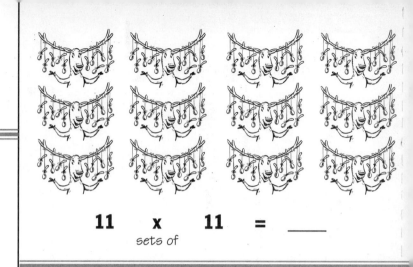

11 x **11** = ___
sets of

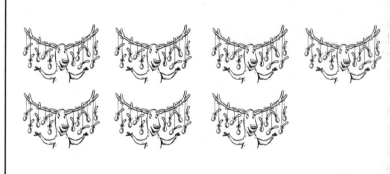

12 x **11** = ___
sets of

❼

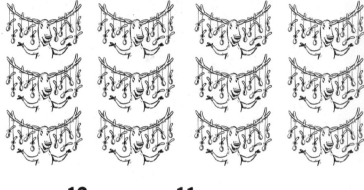

7 x **11** = ___
sets of

8 x **11** = ___
sets of

❺

12 TIMES TABLE MINI-REVIEW

11 x 12 = _____
3 x 12 = _____
10 x 12 = _____
12 x 12 = _____
7 x 12 = _____
5 x 12 = _____
9 x 12 = _____
8 x 12 = _____
2 x 12 = _____
4 x 12 = _____
1 x 12 = _____
6 x 12 = _____

Name: _____

The ⭐12⭐ Times Table

I'm Tillie Tiger.
I've got 12 eggs;
Three beneath
Each of my legs!

Circle each set of 12 eggs inside.

9 x 12 = _____
sets of

3 x 12 = _____
sets of

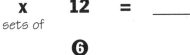

10 x 12 = _____
sets of

4 x 12 = _____
sets of

0 x **12** = **0**
set of

1 x **12** = ___
set of

2 x **12** = ___
sets of

❷

5 x **12** = ___
sets of

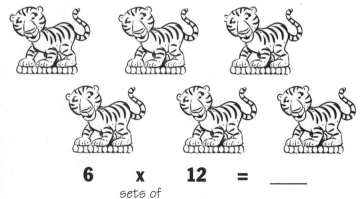

6 x **12** = ___
sets of

❹

11 x **12** = ___
sets of

12 x **12** = ___
sets of

❼

7 x **12** = ___
sets of

8 x **12** = ___
sets of

❺

The 1 Times Table

0 x 1 = 0

1 x 1 = 1

2 x 1 = 2

3 x 1 = 3

4 x 1 = 4

5 x 1 = 5

6 x 1 = 6

7 x 1 = 7

8 x 1 = 8

9 x 1 = 9

10 x 1 = 10

11 x 1 = 11

12 x 1 = 12

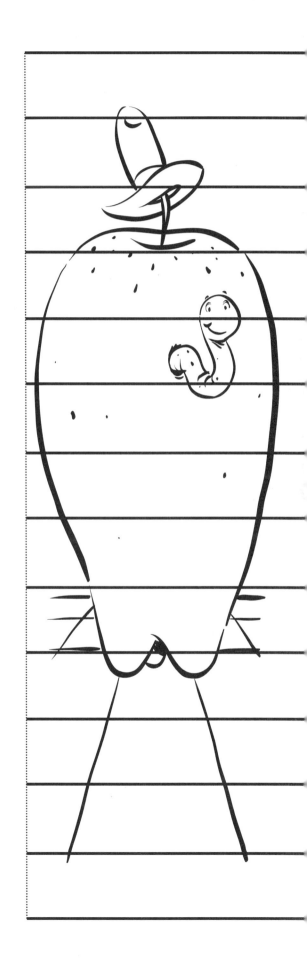

The 2 Times Table

0	x 2 =	0
1	x 2 =	2
2	x 2 =	4
3	x 2 =	6
4	x 2 =	8
5	x 2 =	10
6	x 2 =	12
7	x 2 =	14
8	x 2 =	16
9	x 2 =	18
10	x 2 =	20
11	x 2 =	22
12	x 2 =	24

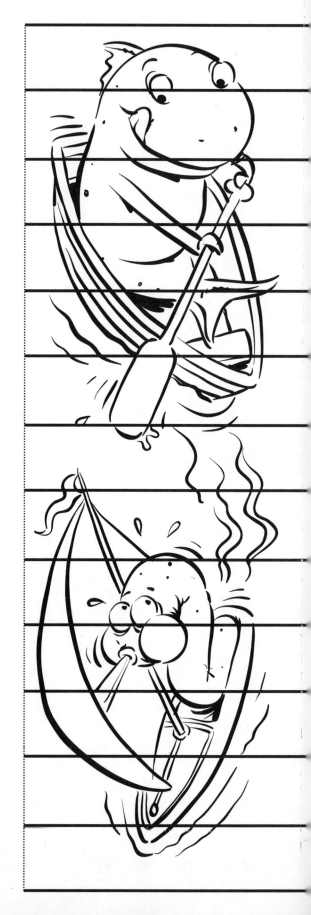

The 3 Times Table

0 x 3 = 0

1 x 3 = 3

2 x 3 = 6

3 x 3 = 9

4 x 3 = 12

5 x 3 = 15

6 x 3 = 18

7 x 3 = 21

8 x 3 = 24

9 x 3 = 27

10 x 3 = 30

11 x 3 = 33

12 x 3 = 36

The 4 Times Table

0 x 4 = 0

1 x 4 = 4

2 x 4 = 8

3 x 4 = 12

4 x 4 = 16

5 x 4 = 20

6 x 4 = 24

7 x 4 = 28

8 x 4 = 32

9 x 4 = 36

10 x 4 = 40

11 x 4 = 44

12 x 4 = 48

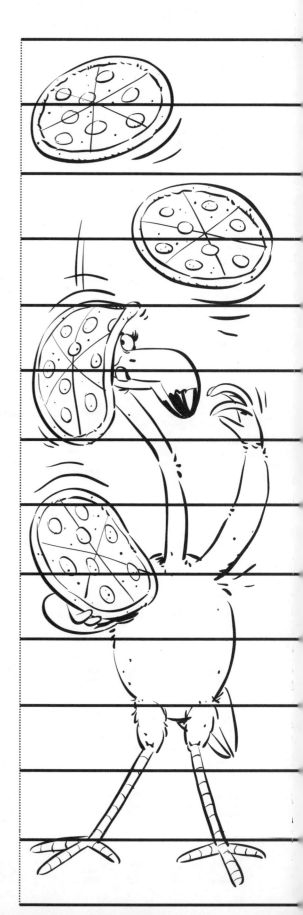

The 5 Times Table

0	x	5	=	0
1	x	5	=	5
2	x	5	=	10
3	x	5	=	15
4	x	5	=	20
5	x	5	=	25
6	x	5	=	30
7	x	5	=	35
8	x	5	=	40
9	x	5	=	45
10	x	5	=	50
11	x	5	=	55
12	x	5	=	60

The 6 Times Table

0 x 6 = 0

1 x 6 = 6

2 x 6 = 12

3 x 6 = 18

4 x 6 = 24

5 x 6 = 30

6 x 6 = 36

7 x 6 = 42

8 x 6 = 48

9 x 6 = 54

10 x 6 = 60

11 x 6 = 66

12 x 6 = 72

The ⑦ Times Table

0 x 7 = 0

1 x 7 = 7

2 x 7 = 14

3 x 7 = 21

4 x 7 = 28

5 x 7 = 35

6 x 7 = 42

7 x 7 = 49

8 x 7 = 56

9 x 7 = 63

10 x 7 = 70

11 x 7 = 77

12 x 7 = 84

The 8 Times Table

0	x	8	=	0
1	x	8	=	8
2	x	8	=	16
3	x	8	=	24
4	x	8	=	32
5	x	8	=	40
6	x	8	=	48
7	x	8	=	56
8	x	8	=	64
9	x	8	=	72
10	x	8	=	80
11	x	8	=	88
12	x	8	=	96

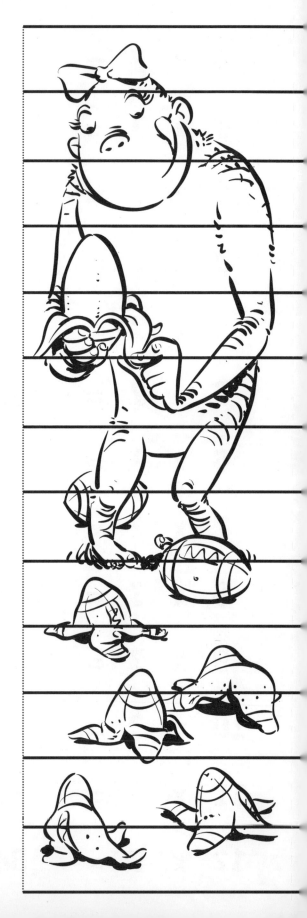

The 9 Times Table

$$0 \times 9 = 0$$

$$1 \times 9 = 9$$

$$2 \times 9 = 18$$

$$3 \times 9 = 27$$

$$4 \times 9 = 36$$

$$5 \times 9 = 45$$

$$6 \times 9 = 54$$

$$7 \times 9 = 63$$

$$8 \times 9 = 72$$

$$9 \times 9 = 81$$

$$10 \times 9 = 90$$

$$11 \times 9 = 99$$

$$12 \times 9 = 108$$

The  10 Times Table

0 x 10 = 0

1 x 10 = 10

2 x 10 = 20

3 x 10 = 30

4 x 10 = 40

5 x 10 = 50

6 x 10 = 60

7 x 10 = 70

8 x 10 = 80

9 x 10 = 90

10 x 10 = 100

11 x 10 = 110

12 x 10 = 120

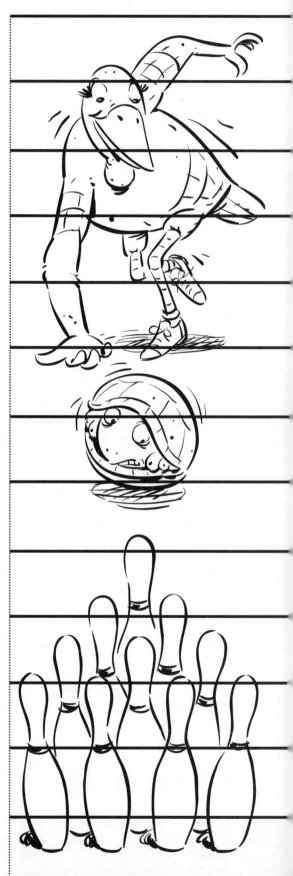

The ⑪ Times Table

0	x 11	=	0
1	x 11	=	11
2	x 11	=	22
3	x 11	=	33
4	x 11	=	44
5	x 11	=	55
6	x 11	=	66
7	x 11	=	77
8	x 11	=	88
9	x 11	=	99
10	x 11	=	110
11	x 11	=	121
12	x 11	=	132

The (12) Times Table

0 x 12 = 0

1 x 12 = 12

2 x 12 = 24

3 x 12 = 36

4 x 12 = 48

5 x 12 = 60

6 x 12 = 72

7 x 12 = 84

8 x 12 = 96

9 x 12 = 108

10 x 12 = 120

11 x 12 = 132

12 x 12 = 144

Multiplication Grid

X	0	1	2	3	4	5	6	7	8	9	10	11	12
0	0	0	0	0	0	0	0	0	0	0	0	0	0
1	0	1	2	3	4	5	6	7	8	9	10	11	12
2	0	2	4	6	8	10	12	14	16	18	20	22	24
3	0	3	6	9	12	15	18	21	24	27	30	33	36
4	0	4	8	12	16	20	24	28	32	36	40	44	48
5	0	5	10	15	20	25	30	35	40	45	50	55	60
6	0	6	12	18	24	30	36	42	48	54	60	66	72
7	0	7	14	21	28	35	42	49	56	63	70	77	84
8	0	8	16	24	32	40	48	56	64	72	80	88	96
9	0	9	18	27	36	45	54	63	72	81	90	99	108
10	0	10	20	30	40	50	60	70	80	90	100	110	120
11	0	11	22	33	44	55	66	77	88	99	110	121	132
12	0	12	24	36	48	60	72	84	96	108	120	132	144

Notes